Meaning *Matters*

Main Idea

Finding Supporting Details

— **Brenda Chapman** —

Grass Roots Press

Meaning Matters: Main Idea
© 2019 Grass Roots Press
www.grassrootsbooks.net

Grass Roots Press acknowledges the financial support
of the Government of Canada for our publishing activities.

Produced with the assistance of the Government of Alberta.

Canada   *Alberta*
          Government

Editor: Dr. Pat Campbell
Image Research: Linda Kita-Bradley

Library and Archives Canada Cataloguing in Publication

Chapman, Brenda, 1955–, author
    Main idea / Brenda Chapman.

(Meaning matters)
ISBN 978-1-77153-235-8 (softcover)

    1. Reading comprehension—Problems, exercises, etc. 2. English
language—Problems, exercises, etc. 3. Reading (Adult education).
I. Title.

LB1050.45.C45 2018   372.47   C2018-901994-8

Printed in Canada

Contents

Main Idea

The main idea is the central or most important idea in a paragraph. Knowing the main idea helps *readers to recall the important information*. The main idea can be explicit or implicit.

Explicit Main idea

An explicit main idea is expressed as a single statement in the paragraph. This statement is usually found in the first or last two sentences of the paragraph.

Implicit Main idea

Sometimes the author does not provide a main idea. This means the reader needs to consider all the details and then produce a single statement that conveys the main idea.

How do I find an explicit main idea?

Check to see if you have found the explicit main idea by following these steps:

❶ Read the paragraph and identify the topic.

❷ Look for a single statement that provides the central idea about the topic.

❸ Find two or three details that support the main idea. If you have found the main idea, it will be easy to find supporting details.

Try it out! *Read this paragraph.*

Giant hogweed can grow up to six metres tall and is covered in clusters of white flowers. This plant is a dangerous weed that releases a toxic sap that can harm a person. The sap causes deep, painful blisters that form within 48 hours. These blisters can persist for weeks. The blisters can leave scars that last for up to six years. The sap also causes long-term sensitivity to sunlight. People need to wear protective clothing if they touch this plant.

❶ What is the topic of the paragraph? _____

❷ Circle the sentence that is the main idea.

❸ Underline two details that support the main idea.

How do I find an implicit main idea?

Check to see if you have found the implicit main idea by following these steps:

❶ Read the paragraph and identify the topic.

❷ Ask yourself two questions:

"What is the author's central message about this topic?"

"What do each of the details of the paragraph have in common?"

❸ Write a sentence that summarizes the main point that the author wants to make about the topic.

❹ Find two or three details that support the main idea. If you have found the main idea, it will be easy to find supporting details.

Try it out! *Read this paragraph.*

Facebook recently announced that it has one billion active users worldwide. It provides a way for people to document their lives. Facebook allows people to connect with far away friends and distant family members. Some people use Facebook because it's a place to share thoughts, causes, and ideas. Some people don't join Facebook because they are concerned about having their privacy invaded. Others find it time consuming. Also, cyberbullying can be a real problem. Despite the drawbacks, Facebook continues to be the world's most famous networking site.

❶ What is the topic of this paragraph? _____

❷ Which of the following is the main idea?

A. Facebook is the world's number one networking site.

B. Facebook, a famous networking site, has benefits and drawbacks.

C. Facebook, a famous networking site, violated people's privacy by sharing data.

❸ Underline two details in the paragraph that support the main idea.

1

Nature *and* Science

Topic: Migration

Many birds migrate to different places, countries and even continents! How do they know where to go? Why don't they get lost? Scientists believe there are several different methods birds use to **navigate**. Some birds have a mineral called magnetite above their beak. This mineral helps birds use the Earth's magnetic field to navigate. Some birds find their way by using landmarks such as rivers or mountains. Birds that migrate during the day use the position of the sun. And those that migrate at night use the moon and the stars. Birds have created their own "maps" to help them navigate.

navigate: to find the way to get to a place.

❶ Underline the sentence in the paragraph that is the main idea.

❷ Which one of the following is *not* a supporting detail?
Circle the correct answer.

A. Birds that migrate at night use the moon and the stars.

B. Many birds migrate to different places, countries and even continents!

C. Some birds find their way by using landmarks such as rivers and mountains.

Topic: African Black Rhino

The African black rhino faces extinction because of **poachers** and consumers. It is estimated that only 2,500 black rhinos remain alive in Africa. Poachers kill the rhino for their horns. Horns are sold for thousands of dollars. Some horns are ground into a fine powder and boiled in water. Some people believe this mixture can be used as medicine to treat illness. Other horns are carved and sold on the black market. People buy knives with handles carved from the horns. It is illegal to hunt black rhinos. But it is unlikely that a law will stop the cycle of supply and demand.

poacher: a person who hunts or fishes for wild animals illegally.

❶ Underline the sentence in the paragraph that is the main idea.

❷ Which one of the following is *not* a supporting detail?
Circle the correct answer.

A. Poachers kill the rhino for their horns.

B. People buy knifes with handles carved from the horns.

C. But it is unlikely that a law will stop the cycle of supply and demand.

DID YOU KNOW?

A drone is a flying robot that can be remotely controlled.

Topic: Drones

What do you call a flying machine without a human pilot? A drone! Drones have many important and exciting purposes. Drones can respond to a disaster such as an earthquake. They can deliver blood and life-saving medical supplies. Drones can also be used in search and rescue missions. An extra set of eyes in the sky can help to find a person lost at sea. Drones are even used to take photos of old bridges. **Engineers** can examine the photos to inspect the safety of the bridge. Drones have fun uses too. Many people use drones to take photos of outdoor events.

engineer: a person who designs and builds products, machines, or structures.

1. Underline the sentence in the paragraph that is the main idea.
2. Which one of the following is *not* a supporting detail? Circle the correct answer.

   A. What do you call a flying machine without a human pilot?

   B. Drones are even used to take photos of old bridges.

   C. They can deliver blood and life-saving medical supplies.

Topic: Electronic Cigarettes (E-cigs)

Around the world, millions of people use e-cigs. Every year, the sale of e-cigs rises. Why are e-cigs so popular? First, many people believe that e-cigs are safer than smoking. But are they? E-cigs release a vapour that people inhale. This vapour does not contain tobacco. But it does contain nicotine and other chemicals. Second, some people use e-cigs as a way to quit smoking. Yet, **vaping** can keep smokers hooked on nicotine. Scientists agree vaping is safer than smoking. But the long-term effects of vaping are not known. The pros and cons should be kept in mind before choosing to vape.

vape: to inhale and exhale the vapour produced by an electronic cigarette.

❶   Underline the sentence in the paragraph that is the main idea.

❷   Which one of the following is *not* a supporting detail?
Circle the correct answer.

   A. Every year, the sale of e-cigs rises.

   B. This vapour does not contain tobacco.

   C. Vaping can keep smokers hooked on nicotine.

DID YOU KNOW?

The Office of Naval Research spent $4 million to study the sixth sense of sailors and Marines.

Topic: The Sixth Sense

Do you make some decisions based on your feelings? If so, you are probably using your sixth sense. It's important to recognize that the sixth sense is a survival system. You could say it's like an alarm. It's important to listen to your sixth sense. When something isn't going well or when you need to respond quickly, the sixth sense is **activated.** Your sixth sense might tell you that you are walking into a dangerous situation. Or your sixth sense might tell you not to take a certain job. The sixth sense is the "spider sense," or uneasy feeling, you cannot explain.

activate: to start working.

❶ Underline the sentence in the paragraph that is the main idea.

❷ Which of the following is *not* a supporting detail?
Circle the correct answer.

   A. Your sixth sense might tell you not to take a certain job.

   B. The sixth sense is the "spider sense," or uneasy feeling, you cannot explain.

   C. Your sixth sense might tell you that you are walking into a dangerous situation.

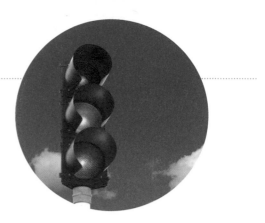

Topic: Colour Blindness

Colour blindness is a condition that affects men more than women. Colour-blind people face many difficulties in everyday life. Red-green colour **deficiency** is the most common form of colour blindness. People who cannot distinguish between those colours might mix up traffic lights. This can make driving difficult, especially at night. Colour-blind people can get sunburns because they cannot see their skin turning red. Even cooking can pose problems. For example, it can be difficult to tell if a steak is rare or well done. And selecting produce can be a challenge. A green banana might look the same as a ripe one!

deficiency: a lack of something that is needed.

1. Underline the sentence in the paragraph that is the main idea.

2. Which one of the following is *not* a supporting detail?
Circle the correct answer.

A. Colour blindness can make driving difficult, especially at night.

B. Colour blindness is a condition that affects men more than women.

C. Colour-blind people can get sunburns because they cannot see their skin turning red.

DID YOU KNOW?

*A coral reef is a ridge of rock
in the sea formed by the growth
and deposit of coral.*

Topic: Coral Reefs

Coral reefs are the jewels of the ocean. Their beauty is matched by their fragility. Did you know that 50% of the world's coral reefs have died? The biggest global threat to coral reefs is climate change. Warmer oceans cause a condition called **coral bleaching**. This bleaching causes corals to lose the **algae** living in their tissues. The corals need the algae—it is their main food source. In order to stay healthy, local threats must also be controlled. For example, pollution from coastal towns finds its way into coral reefs. This pollution includes sewage and plastic debris.

algae: simple plants with no leaves or stems that grow in or near water.
coral bleaching: a process which causes corals to lose their colour.

❶ Which of the following is the main idea?
Circle the correct answer.

A. Coral reefs need to be protected.

B. Coral reefs are dying from lack of food.

C. Coral reefs are dying from climate change and pollution.

❷ Underline two supporting details in the paragraph.

Photo: © Bigstock

2

People

DID YOU KNOW?

*Florence Nightingale was a pioneer
in the field of nursing.*

Topic: Florence Nightingale (1820 – 1910)

In the 1800s, women were expected to marry. But Florence Nightingale chose a different path. She believed her purpose in life was to become a nurse. Her first job was in a British hospital. In 1854, she took volunteer nurses to the **Crimean War**. Florence and her nurses saved many lives. She returned home and opened the first school to train nurses. She wrote a book with new nursing methods. The poor received treatment for the first time. Many patients lived who would have died. Florence Nightingale's path led to a nursing career and better health care for patients.

Crimean War (1853-1856): A war fought by Britain, France and Turkey against Russia.

❶   Underline the sentence in the paragraph that is the main idea.

❷   Which one of the following is *not* a supporting detail?
    Circle the correct answer.

    A. In the 1800s, women were expected to marry.

    B. Florence opened the first school to train nurses.

    C. Florence wrote a book with new nursing methods.

DID YOU KNOW?

*Bill Gates founded Microsoft,
the largest computer software
company in the world.*

Topic: Bill Gates (1955 –)

As a 13-year-old student, Bill Gates was introduced to computers.
Bill did well in school, but he was bored. Bill dropped out of college in
1975. Bill wanted to start a software company. Bill and a partner founded
Microsoft. The company became a business success. Today, Bill Gates is
one of the richest men in the world. Bill and his wife started a **foundation.**
They donated $28 billion to their foundation. This foundation does work
around the world. The money is used to support health and education.
Bill, co-founder of Microsoft, is a wealthy man with a big heart.

foundation: an organization that is funded by people's donations
and helps society.

❶ Underline the sentence in the paragraph that is the main idea.

❷ Which one of the following is *not* a supporting detail?
Circle the correct answer.

   A. They donated $28 billion to their foundation.

   B. Bill Gates is one of the richest men in the world.

   C. As a 13-year-old student, Bill Gates was introduced to computers.

Topic: Ernest Shackleton (1874 – 1922)

Ernest Shackleton had a dream. He wanted to sail to the South Pole. In 1914, Ernest and his crew departed for the South Pole. In January 1915, their ship became trapped in ice. Ernest and his crew set up camp on the drifting ice. In April, Ernest and 27 crew members crowded into three small life boats. They sailed to a **deserted** island. From there, Shackleton and five crew members took a 750-mile journey by life boat to find help. A rescue team helped save the men on the deserted island. Shackleton saved his crew, but his dream did not come true.

deserted: having no people.

① Underline the sentence in the paragraph that is the main idea.

② Which one of the following is *not* a supporting detail?
Circle the correct answer.

    A. Ernest wanted to sail to the South Pole.

    B. In January 1915, their ship became trapped in ice.

    C. Shackleton and five crew members took a 750-mile journey by lifeboat to find help.

Celia Cruz, the Queen of **Salsa**, *won three Grammy Awards for her music.*

Topic: Celia Cruz (1925 – 2003)

Celia Cruz was the most popular Latin artist of the 20th century. Celia was raised in Cuba. Her parents wanted her to become a teacher. Celia studied education, but her passion was singing. She entered a radio singing contest and won first prize. Celia returned to school to study music. Then, she got a big break. A band called Sonora Matancera asked Celia to be their lead singer. Celia sang with the band for 15 years. Soon, Celia was more famous than the band. By the time Celia died in 2003, she had 23 gold albums and many awards.

salsa: a type of popular Latin American music and dance.

1. Underline the sentence in the paragraph that is the main idea.

2. Which one of the following is *not* a supporting detail?
Circle the correct answer.

A. Celia was more famous than the band.

B. Her parents wanted her to become a teacher.

C. Celia had 23 gold albums and many awards.

Topic: Pitseolak Ashoona (1904 – 1983)

Pitseolak was born in 1904. She married an Inuit hunter. They had 17 children. After Pitseolak's husband died, she faced many years of hardship. Pitseolak felt all alone. She taught herself to draw and make prints. She drew in pencil crayons, felt-tipped pens, and **graphite.** Pitseolak sold her first set of drawings for $20. The sale of her artwork supported her family. Her artwork was based on stories from her life. Most of the artwork was based on good memories. Pitseolak produced more than 9,000 drawings. Pitseolak's art helped her move from tragedy to triumph.

graphite: a form of carbon that leaves a shiny metallic grey color on a surface when moved across it.

❶ Underline the sentence in the paragraph that is the main idea.

❷ Which one of the following is *not* a supporting detail?
Circle the correct answer.

A. Pitseolak married an Inuit hunter.

B. The sale of her artwork supported her family.

C. After Pitseolak's husband died, she faced many years of hardship.

Topic: Harvey Milk (1930 – 1978)

Harvey Milk was a **civil rights** leader who was killed for his beliefs. In the 1950s, gay men did not have the rights of other men. Gay men were excluded from many workplaces. For example, they could not work for the government. In 1973, Harvey ran for city council. He wanted gay people to have equal rights. He lost the election. He ran two more times and lost. In 1977, Harvey was elected. As a civil rights leader, he worked hard for his community. Harvey was shot and killed 11 months after taking office. Many people still view Harvey as a hero.

civil rights: the rights that all people have to equal treatment and opportunities.

❶ Underline the sentence in the paragraph that is the main idea.

❷ Which one of the following is *not* a supporting detail? Circle the correct answer.

A. Harvey wanted gay people to have equal rights.

B. Gay men were excluded from many workplaces.

C. Harvey was shot and killed 11 months after taking office.

DID YOU KNOW?

Jackie Robinson was an important figure in baseball and the Civil Rights movement.

Topic: Jackie Robinson (1919 – 1972)

In 1947, the Brooklyn Dodgers signed Jackie to play first base. He was the first black man to play Major League Baseball. He won the **Rookie** of the Year award. In 1949, Jackie won the Most Valuable Player award for the National League. He was the first black player to win this award in any major league sport. Before retiring, Jackie became the highest-paid athlete in Dodgers history. He retired from baseball in 1956. He was hired by a TV station. Jackie became the first black man to cover Major League Baseball on TV. Jackie made history by breaking through baseball's colour barrier.

rookie: a first-year player in a professional sport.

❶ Which of the following is the main idea?
Circle the correct answer.

A. Jackie enjoyed many firsts in his career.

B. Jackie is famous because of his baseball career.

C. Jackie Robinson will always be remembered for breaking through the colour barrier.

❷ Underline two supporting details in the paragraph.

3

Health

DID YOU KNOW?

In a sweat lodge, hot stones heat the room to 102° F.

Topic: _____ _____

The sweat lodge ceremony is a Native tradition that follows many **rituals.** The ceremony takes place in a dome-shaped structure called a sweat lodge. Prior to entering the lodge, participants smudge their body with sage or sweet grass. A spiritual leader conducts the sweat lodge ceremony. Sometimes, the leader is a Native elder. People gather around a pit filled with heated stones. Water is poured on the hot stones to create steam. A sweat lodge ceremony typically has four sessions that are called rounds. Each round, which lasts 30 to 45 minutes, increases in heat. People cleanse their bodies and minds during a sweat.

ritual: a formal ceremony or series of acts that is always performed in the same way.

① What is the topic of this paragraph? Write the topic in the space provided.

② Underline the sentence in the paragraph that is the main idea.

③ Which one of the following is *not* a supporting detail?
Circle the correct answer.

   A. People cleanse their bodies and minds during a sweat.

   B. A sweat lodge ceremony typically has four sessions that are called rounds.

   C. Prior to entering the lodge, participants smudge their body with sage or sweet grass.

Adults need between seven and nine hours of sleep per night to function at their best.

Topic: _____

One of the best ways to feel good is free! The power of sleep is the key to happiness and good health. One of the most active parts of your body during sleep is your brain. A good night's sleep helps you to focus, learn, and retain information. As well, sleep leads to better decision-making. Sleep also boosts your body's **immune system**, which helps to fight colds and flu bugs. Sleep is also connected to our emotions. A good night's sleep improves your mood and your ability to handle stress. Your friends and family will notice when you've enjoyed a good sleep.

immune system: the system that protects the body from disease by producing antibodies.

① What is the topic of this paragraph? Write the topic in the space provided.

② Underline the sentence that is the main idea.

③ Which of the following is *not* a supporting detail?
Circle the correct answer.

A. Sleep also helps to boost your body's immune system.

B. One of the most active parts of your body during sleep is your brain.

C. A good night's sleep improves your mood and your ability to handle stress.

DID YOU KNOW?

Cholera is a disease of the small intestine caused by infected water supplies.

Topic: _____ _____

Yemen is the poorest country in the Middle East. In 2017, Yemen's civil war caused the worst cholera outbreak in history. The war caused water treatment plants to shut down. People did not have access to clean drinking water. People drank water that contained the cholera **bacteria**. Treatment can save lives. But the war destroyed Yemen's health care system. There were not enough health care workers. And medicine was in short supply. There were over one million cases of cholera. More than 2,200 people died. By 2018, people had access to a cholera vaccine.

bacteria: a very small organism found in air, soil, and water that can cause disease.

❶ What is the topic of this paragraph? Write the topic in the space provided.

❷ Underline the sentence that is the main idea.
Circle the correct answer.

❸ Which of the following is *not* a supporting detail?

A. The war destroyed Yemen's health care system.

B. By 2018, people had access to a cholera vaccine.

C. People drank water that contained the cholera bacteria.

Photo: © Alamy

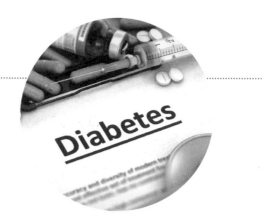

Topic: _____

There are several common symptoms of diabetes. These symptoms are caused by a high level of sugar in the bloodstream. An early warning sign is an unusual thirst. A person with diabetes also needs to go to the restroom more often. Sometimes, **blurred** vision is a symptom. A person with diabetes can lose or gain weight with no change in diet. They might be tired and lack energy. A bruise or cut could take a long time to heal. There could be tingling in the hands or feet. Sometimes, there are no symptoms. A simple blood test can indicate if a person has diabetes.

blurred: difficult to see.

1. What is the topic of this paragraph? Write the topic in the space provided.

2. Underline the sentence that is the main idea.

3. Which of the following is *not* a supporting detail?
   Circle the correct answer.

   A. Sometimes, blurred vision is a symptom.

   B. A bruise or cut could take a long time to heal.

   C. These symptoms are caused by a high level of sugar in the bloodstream.

CHANGE YOUR CLOCKS

DID YOU KNOW?

Daylight saving time involves setting clocks one hour forward in the spring.

Topic: _____

Every spring, people in North America prepare for daylight saving time (DST). They advance their clocks one hour before going to sleep. The next day, the sun rises and sets an hour later. Some people complain because they lose an hour of sleep and feel tired. DST **disrupts** their internal body clock. It takes about a day to adjust to this hour of time change. Other people enjoy DST. The spring weather feels warmer and the days seem longer. People can enjoy outdoor activities well into the evening hours. People can spend more time enjoying outdoor activities in the evening. DST presents both benefits and challenges for people.

disrupt: to cause (something) to be unable to continue in the normal way.

❶ What is the topic of this paragraph? Write the topic in the space provided.

❷ Underline the sentence that is the main idea.

❸ Which of the following is *not* a supporting detail?
Circle the correct answer.

A. DST disrupts their internal body clock.

B. The next day, the sun rises and sets an hour later.

C. People can spend more time enjoying outdoor activities in the evening.

27

Doctors Without Borders (DWB) is a non-profit group that provides medical supplies and treatment to people in distress.

Topic: _____

Doctors Without Borders (DWB) sends health care workers to over 60 countries. This group responds to a variety of health care challenges around the world. They help victims of disasters such as floods. DWB is able to respond quickly to a disaster. It also provides health care to people suffering from diseases. For example, they provide health care to people with cholera. As well, they provide vaccines to prevent an outbreak of disease. Finally, DWB also provides health care to victims of armed conflict. DWB finds it difficult to recruit staff who can work on a range of health issues.

❶ What is the topic of this paragraph? Write the topic in the space provided.

❷ Underline the sentence that is the main idea.

❸ Which of the following is *not* a supporting detail?
Circle the correct answer.

A. DWB helps victims of disasters such as floods.

B. DWB provides health care to people suffering from diseases.

C. DWB finds it difficult to recruit staff who can work on a range of health issues.

DID YOU KNOW?

Therapy dogs visit people in hospitals, nursing homes, and schools.

Topic: _____

A therapy dog is a friend to everyone! These dogs are patient and gentle, just like a best friend. Therapy dogs accept all people. They do not make judgements based on age, appearance, or language. Therapy dogs offer affection and comfort to those in need. They provide emotional support to people who feel lonely, anxious, or depressed. Spending time with a therapy dog helps to calm people. Therapy dogs interact with people in many ways. They sit beside people and listen to their stories. They jump on people's laps for a big hug! Therapy dogs accept and support children and adults who need a friend.

❶ What is the topic of this paragraph? Write the topic in the space provided.

❷ Which of the following is the main idea?
Circle the correct answer.

A. Therapy dogs like to spend time with people.

B. Therapy dogs provide friendship to everyone.

C. Therapy dogs help people feel better during hard times.

❸ Underline two supporting details in the paragraph.

Photo: © Bigstock

4

Environment

DID YOU KNOW?

*Delhi, the capital of India,
is one of the most polluted cities
in the world.*

Topic: _____

Delhi is usually covered by a blanket of **toxic** smog. Much of the smog
comes from nearby farms that burn crop stubble. Car exhaust vapour adds
to the smog. The smog gets worse in the winter due to lower temperatures.
People who live in Delhi can get sick from breathing the air. In fact,
breathing Delhi air is like smoking 50 cigarettes a day. People deal with
the smog by staying indoors. Some grow indoor plants to cleanse the air.
Others use face masks when they go outside. People deal with Delhi's smog
in different ways in order to avoid getting sick.

toxic: poisonous.

❶ What is the topic of this paragraph? Write the topic in the space provided.

❷ Underline the sentence in the paragraph that is the main idea.

❸ Which one of the following is *not* a supporting detail?
    Circle the correct answer.

    A. People use face masks when they go outside.

    B. Some people grow indoor plants to cleanse the air.

    C. Much of the smog comes from nearby farms that burn crop stubble.

Photo: © Bigstock

Topic: _____

The **banning** of plastic bags will help to protect the environment and wildlife. Every year, millions of plastic bags end up in landfills. Over time, the bags release toxic chemicals into the ground. Millions of other bags end up in the ocean. Wildlife mistake plastic bags for food. The bags can choke or poison sea life and birds. Some cities and towns have banned plastic bags. In Canada, Montreal was the first major city to ban plastic bags. And San Francisco was the first major U.S. city to ban plastic bags. People are learning to use cloth bags when they shop.

ban: to forbid.

❶ What is the topic of this paragraph? Write the topic in the space provided.

❷ Underline the sentence in the paragraph that is the main idea.

❸ Which one of the following is *not* a supporting detail?
Circle the correct answer.

A. The bags can choke or poison sea life and birds.

B. The bags release toxic chemicals into the ground.

C. Some cities and towns have banned plastic bags.

DID YOU KNOW?

*A wind farm is a group
of wind turbines.*

Topic: _____

There are thousands of wind farms around the world. The wind turbines change the wind's energy into electricity. Wind farms are easy to maintain, unlike other power sources. And the turbines are a cheap source of energy that does not create any pollution. Some families who live near wind farms have made formal complaints. They complain that wind turbines sound like a jet that never lands. The noise prevents sleep and causes headaches. Others are upset because birds that fly into the turbines' blades can be killed. Wind turbines provide clean, cheap energy, but have some drawbacks.

❶ What is the topic of this paragraph? Write the topic in the space provided.

❷ Underline the sentence in the paragraph that is the main idea.

❸ Which one of the following is *not* a supporting detail?
Circle the correct answer.

A. The noise prevents sleep and causes headaches.

B. There are thousands of wind farms around the world.

C. Wind farms are easy to maintain, unlike other power sources.

DID YOU KNOW?

An electric car uses energy stored in its rechargeable batteries.

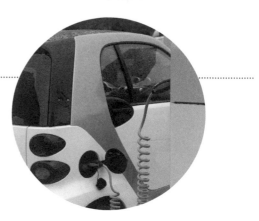

Topic: _____

Many people want to buy electric cars. Why are these cars so popular? First, people want to save money on fuel and repair costs. This is usually the main reason to purchase an electric car. And second, people want to protect the environment. Electric cars do not **emit** toxic vapours. Still, there are some drawbacks to consider. An electric car costs more than a gas-powered car. And you need to spend time planning your route. Recharging stations are more difficult to find than gas stations. People need to consider the pros and cons before buying an electric car.

emit: to send (light, energy, etc.) out from a source.

1. What is the topic of this paragraph? Write the topic in the space provided.

2. Underline the sentence in the paragraph that is the main idea.

3. Which one of the following is *not* a supporting detail?
Circle the correct answer.

   A. Many people want to buy electric cars.

   B. Electric cars do not emit toxic vapours.

   C. Recharging stations are more difficult to find than gas stations.

DID YOU KNOW?

Houses in Switzerland are built to support roof top gardens.

Topic: _____

Today, many home owners are discovering the benefits of rooftop gardens. A bare roof can get as hot as 158° F on a sunny day. But the same roof, when covered by a roof garden, is around 77° F. The roof garden provides shade. People do not turn on the **A/C** because their homes are cooler. This results in big energy savings. Another benefit to roof gardens is their ability to manage rainfall. After a rain storm, the roof garden absorbs much of the water. The roof garden reduces the amount of water runoff by 75%. This eases the burden on local storm sewer systems.

A/C: air conditioning.

① What is the topic of this paragraph? Write the topic in the space provided.

② Underline the sentence in the paragraph that is the main idea.

③ Which one of the following is *not* a supporting detail?
Circle the correct answer.

A. The roof garden provides shade.

B. A bare roof can get as hot as 158° F on a sunny day.

C. The roof garden reduces the amount of runoff by 75%.

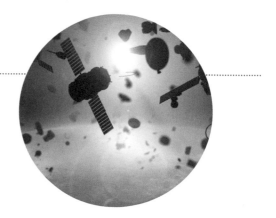

Space junk is man-made rubbish floating in space.

Topic: _____

If you look at the sky on a clear night, you will see many stars. You might also be looking at pieces of junk. The amount of debris in space is a growing problem. The U.S. Space Agency estimates there are 750,000 pieces of space debris. The debris ranges in size from 1 cm to the size of a fridge. In addition, there are over 150 million tiny fragments. The space debris travels at speeds of up to 17,500 miles per hour. The debris can cause severe damage. Even a piece the size of a marble can damage spacecraft and satellites.

debris: the pieces that are left after something has been destroyed.

❶ What is the topic of this paragraph? Write the topic in the space provided.

❷ Underline the sentence in the paragraph that is the main idea.

❸ Which one of the following is *not* a supporting detail?
Circle the correct answer.

A. The debris can cause severe damage.

B. There are over 150 million tiny fragments.

C. If you look at the sky on a clear night, you will see many stars.

DID YOU KNOW?

Experts used to think that nuclear power would change the world for the better.

Topic: _____ _____

In 1977, the Chernobyl Nuclear Power Plant was built in Pripyat. The plant supplied electrical power to Ukraine. In 1986, the plant exploded. The blast killed two workers. A second later, there was another blast. Then, the plant began to burn. **Radiation** entered the air. It spread near and far. Many firemen fighting the blaze were sent to hospital. Six of the firemen died from the radiation. After the disaster, Pripyat turned into a ghost town. About 50,000 people left their homes. How many people died? Nobody knows. The long-term health effects are not known. But over 7,000 children developed thyroid cancer.

radiation: a type of dangerous and powerful energy that is produced by nuclear reactions.

❶ What is the topic of this paragraph? Write the topic in the space provided.

❷ Which of the following is the main idea?
Circle the correct answer.

A. The Chernobyl explosion killed many people.

B. The Chernobyl Nuclear Power Plant supplied electrical power to Ukraine.

C. The Chernobyl explosion was a disaster that proved the dangers of using nuclear power.

❸ Underline two supporting details in the paragraph.

Photo: © iStock

5

History

DID YOU KNOW?

Mahatma Gandhi, leader of India's independence movement, used non-violent methods to protest.

Topic: _____

In 1930, Britain ruled India. Mahatma Gandhi's Salt March was a peaceful protest against British rule and laws. Under British law, Indian citizens could not collect or sell salt. They were forced to buy salt from Britain. The cost of that salt was too high. In protest, Gandhi led a 240-mile march to the sea. Gandhi wanted to make salt from sea water. But the British police stopped him. Gandhi picked up a lump of salt from the mud. This simple act **defied** British law. Soon thousands of people across India joined Gandhi in peaceful protest. In time, Gandhi's leadership helped India gain independence.

defy: to refuse to obey.

1. What is the topic of this paragraph? Write the topic in the space provided.
2. Underline the sentence in the paragraph that is the main idea.
3. Which one of the following is *not* a supporting detail?
   Circle the correct answer.

   A. The cost of the salt was too high.

   B. Gandhi led a 240-mile march to the sea.

   C. Thousands of people across India joined Gandhi in peaceful protest.

The builder of the Titanic, a luxury steamship, believed that it was unsinkable.

Topic: _____

The *Titanic* struck an iceberg during her **maiden** voyage. Human error played a big part in the tragedy. Other passing ships had warned the Titanic about large chunks of floating ice. The warnings were ignored. The captain kept the *Titanic* going at full speed. On April 14, 1912, the ship hit an iceberg at 11:40 p.m. The ship started to sink. There were not enough lifeboats. The crew was not well trained. They put the lifeboats into the water. Many of the lifeboats were not filled to capacity. More than 700 people were saved. But more than 1,500 people drowned.

maiden: first

❶ What is the topic of this paragraph? Write the topic in the space provided.

❷ Underline the sentence in the paragraph that is the main idea.

❸ Which one of the following is *not* a supporting detail?
Circle the correct answer.

A. The warnings were ignored.

B. The crew was not well trained.

C. They put the lifeboats in the water.

DID YOU KNOW?

*Many Prairie settlers built homes made from **sod**.*

Topic: _____ _____

Can you imagine living in a house made from sod? These houses, built by Prairie settlers, were called soddies. They were difficult to build and live in. First, the settlers dug out a cellar by hand. Then they used a special plough to cut sod into blocks. They stacked hundreds of blocks by hand. The soddy was dark inside. The air was stale. Mice and insects lived in the sod. Dirt fell and water dripped from the sod ceilings. Sometimes, the soddy collapsed from heavy winds and rain. Settlers built soddies from the 1800s up until World War I.

sod: the upper layer of soil that is made up of grass and plant roots.

❶ What is the topic of this paragraph? Write the topic in the space provided.

❷ Underline the sentence in the paragraph that is the main idea.

❸ Which one of the following is *not* a supporting detail?
Circle the correct answer.

A. They stacked hundreds of blocks by hand.

B. Dirt fell and water dripped from the sod ceilings.

C. Settlers built soddies from the 1800s up until World War I.

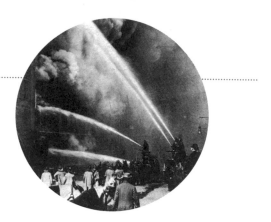

In the early 1900s, garment factories employed people who worked long hours for low wages.

Topic: _____

In 1911, the Triangle Shirtwaist Factory in New York caught fire. The fire started on the 8th floor. It caused the deaths of 146 garment workers. Most of the victims were young immigrant women. The owners had locked the doors. They did that to prevent theft. The workers were trapped inside and many died in the fire. Others died jumping from the burning building. The Triangle Shirtwaist Factory fire was a tragic event that could have been prevented. The tragedy brought attention to **sweatshop** conditions. The fire led to a law requiring factory owners to improve safety standards for their workers.

sweatshop: a place where people work long hours for low pay in poor conditions.

1   What is the topic of this paragraph? Write the topic in the space provided.

2   Underline the sentence in the paragraph that is the main idea.

3   Which one of the following is *not* a supporting detail?
Circle the correct answer.

    A. The owners had locked the doors.

    B. The fire caused the deaths of 146 garment workers.

    C. The tragedy brought attention to sweatshop conditions.

In 1969, young people gathered for four days of music in Woodstock, New York.

Topic: _____

Woodstock was a music festival held in a hayfield. The event planners expected about 50,000 people. Much to their surprise, over 500,000 people came to hear the music. Traffic jams filled the highways and people abandoned their cars. The event planners were not prepared for such a large crowd. By the second day, the festival had run out of food. Heavy rain created a muddy mess in the hayfield. People and their belongings were caked in mud. There were no showers and not enough **portable** toilets. Thousands of people left before the event ended. But those who stayed still remember the music.

portable: easy to move around.

❶ What is the topic of this paragraph? Write the topic in the space provided.

❷ Underline the sentence in the paragraph that is the main idea.

❸ Which one of the following is *not* a supporting detail? Circle the correct answer.

A. Thousands of people left before the event ended.

B. The event planners expected about 50,000 people.

C. By the second day, the festival had run out of food.

Home children is a term used to describe children who migrated from Britain to Canada.

Topic: _____

British charity groups sent more than 100,000 children to Canada. These children migrated between 1869 and 1939. Most children came from poor families. A few were orphans. These children were supposed to be going to a better life. But this did not happen. Home children became a source of cheap labour. Many of the older ones worked as unpaid farm workers. Others worked as servants. Most worked long hours under hard conditions. The children's needs were not met. For example, many children received little or no education. The home children program had good **intentions,** but did not provide children with a better life.

intention: the thing that you plan to do or achieve.

❶ What is the topic of this paragraph? Write the topic in the space provided.

❷ Underline the sentence in the paragraph that is the main idea.

❸ Which one of the following is *not* a supporting detail?
Circle the correct answer.

A. These children migrated between 1869 and 1939.

B. These children were supposed to be going to a better life.

C. Many of the older children worked as unpaid farm workers.

The women's **suffrage** *movement gave women the right to vote.*

Topic: _____

In the early 1900s, women were not allowed to vote in Canada. Women were supposed to take care of the house. Women were supposed to raise children. Women leaders saw this as wrong. These leaders were called suffragists. They believed women should have the same rights as men. Women should be allowed to vote. The suffragists lobbied governments to change the voting laws. The suffragists fought until women won the right to vote. By 1921, women could vote in Canada's federal election. But not all women. Asian women could not vote until 1948. First Nations women could not vote until 1960.

suffrage: the right of women to vote in political elections.

❶ What is the topic of this paragraph? Write the topic in the space provided.

❷ Which of the following is the main idea?
Circle the correct answer.

A. Women were supposed to take care of the house and their children.

B. Asian and First Nations women were not given the right to vote in 1921.

C. The suffragists convinced governments that women had the right to vote.

❸ Underline two supporting details in the paragraph.

Photo: © Alamy

Answer Key

Introduction

Page 4:
1. Topic: giant hogweed; a toxic weed
2. This plant is a dangerous weed that releases a toxic sap that can harm a person.

Page 5:
1. Topic: Facebook
2. B

Unit 1: Nature & Science

Page 7
1. Scientists believe there are several different methods birds use to navigate.
2. B

Page 8
1. The African black rhino faces extinction because of poachers and consumers.
2. C

Page 9
1. Drones have many important and exciting purposes.
2. A

Page 10
1. The pros and cons should be kept in mind before choosing to vape.
2. A

Page 11
1. It's important to recognize that the sixth sense is a survival system.
2. B

Page 12
1. Colour-blind people face many difficulties in everyday life.
2. B

Page 13
1. C

Unit 2: People

Page 15
1. Florence Nightingale's path led to a nursing career and better health care for patients.
2. A

Page 16
1. Bill, co-founder of Microsoft, is a wealthy man with a big heart.
2. C

Page 17
1. Shackleton saved his crew but his dream did not come true.
2. B

Page 18
1. Celia Cruz was the most popular Latin artist of the 20th century.
2. B

Page 19
❶ Pitseolak's art helped her move
   from tragedy to triumph.
❷ A

Page 20
❶ Harvey Milk was a civil rights leader
   who was killed for his beliefs.
❷ B

Page 21
❶ A

Unit 3: Health

Page 23
❶ sweat lodge ceremony
❷ The sweat lodge ceremony is a Native
   tradition that follows many rituals.
❸ A

Page 24
❶ sleep; benefits of sleep; power of sleep
❷ The power of sleep is the key
   to happiness and good health.
❸ B

Page 25
❶ cholera; cholera outbreak;
   cholera in Yemen
❷ In 2017, Yemen's civil war caused
   the worst cholera outbreak in history.
❸ B

Page 26
❶ diabetes; symptoms of diabetes
❷ There are several common symptoms
   of diabetes.
❸ C

Page 27
❶ Daylight saving time
❷ DST presents both benefits
   and challenges for people.
❸ B

Page 28
❶ Doctors Without Borders
❷ This group responds to a variety of
   health care challenges around the world.
❸ C

Page 29
❶ therapy dogs
❷ C

Unit 4: Environment

Page 31
❶ smog; toxic smog; Delhi's smog
❷ People deal with Delhi's smog in different
   ways in order to avoid getting sick.
❸ C

Page 32
❶ banning plastic bags
❷ The banning of plastic bags will help
   to protect the environment and wildlife.
❸ C

Page 33

❶ wind farm; wind turbines

❷ Wind turbines provide clean, cheap energy, but have some drawbacks.

❸ B

Page 34

❶ electric cars

❷ People need to consider the pros and cons before buying an electric car.

❸ A

Page 35

❶ rooftop gardens

❷ Today, many home owners are discovering the benefits of rooftop gardens.

❸ B

Page 36

❶ space junk; space debris

❷ The amount of debris in space is a growing problem.

❸ C

Page 37

❶ The Chernobyl explosion; The Chernobyl Nuclear Power Plant

❷ C

Unit 5: History

Page 39:

❶ The Salt March, Gandhi's Salt March

❷ Mahatma Gandhi's Salt March was a peaceful protest against British rule and laws.

❸ A

Page 40:

❶ The *Titanic*; the sinking of the *Titanic*

❷ Human error played a big part in the tragedy.

❸ C

Page 41:

❶ soddies; the soddy

❷ They were difficult to build and live in.

❸ C

Page 42:

❶ Triangle Shirtwaist Factory; the factory fire

❷ The Triangle Shirtwaist Factory fire was a tragic event that could have been prevented.

❸ C

Page 43:

❶ Woodstock; music festival

❷ The event planners were not prepared for such a large crowd.

❸ A

Page 44:

❶ home children

❷ The home children program had good intentions, but did not provide children with a better life.

❸ A

Page 45:

❶ suffrage movement; suffragists; the right to vote

❷ C